I0804135

A Cold Cube

by Julianna Mueller
illustrated by C. A. Nobens

Practice Decodable 17

McGraw Hill Education

Bothell, WA • Chicago, IL • Columbus, OH • New York, NY

MHEonline.com

Copyright © 2015 McGraw-Hill Education

All rights reserved. No part of this publication may be reproduced or distributed in any form or by any means, or stored in a database or retrieval system, without the prior written consent of McGraw-Hill Education, including, but not limited to, network storage or transmission, or broadcast for distance learning.

Send all inquiries to:
McGraw-Hill Education
8787 Orion Place
Columbus, OH 43240

ISBN: 978-0-02-145061-9
MHID: 0-02-145061-7

Printed in China.

8 9 10 11 12 DSS 27 26 25 24 23

Abe has a big, cold cube.

What can Abe do with a cube?

Can Abe make a cute little pig?

Can Abe make a cute mule?

What did Abe do with a cube?

Abe made a cute, little man!